THIS CITY
AND OTHER POEMS

Published by Spinner Publications, Inc.
P.O. Box 1801 · New Bedford, MA 02741

©Copyright 1999 by Everett Hoagland. All rights reserved.

Printed in the United States of America
Third Printing

Manuscript Typist: Kamal E. Hoagland

Cover Painting: Milton H. Brightman,
"Snow Fall at the Hurricane Barrier," 1993

THIS CITY
AND OTHER POEMS

BY

EVERETT HOAGLAND

Spinner Publications, Inc.
New Bedford, Massachusetts

Acknowledgments

Poetry chapbooks by Everett Hoagland:
 Ten Poems, 1968
 Black Velvet, 1970
 Scrimshaw, 1976

Some of the following poems, sometimes in different forms, first appeared in the following publications:

The American Poetry Review

Compass

Discover America: San Jose Studies, San Jose University

First World

The Massachusetts Review

The Standard-Times, New Bedford

Scrimshaw, published by Patmos Press

Temper, The UMass Dartmouth Literary Review

Some of these poems were recently written and/or read for/at the following as a public service:

The Martha Briggs Club Beautillion 1995 –
   Seaport Inn, Fairhaven, MA

The Unveiling of The Frederick Douglass Memorial Plaque – City Hall, New Bedford, MA

The Annual A. I. D. S. Awareness Program –
   Buttonwood Park, New Bedford, MA

The Opening Reception For The Frederick Douglass Unity House – UMass Dartmouth, Dartmouth, MA

The Anniversary Celebration for the Friends of The New Bedford Public Libraries – New Bedford, MA

Two New Bedford Minority Action Coalition Benefit Programs – The Cape Verdean Veterans Association, New Bedford, MA

A Benefit for the Market Ministries Homeless Shelter –
   Days Inn, New Bedford, MA

The "Three Generations of African American Poets" Program – Bethel A. M. E. Church, New Bedford, MA

The "New Bedford Poets Celebrate The City" – Program for The New Bedford Sesquicentennial Celebration, Seamens Bethel, Johnny Cake Hill, New Bedford, MA

The Annual Writers Harvest For The Hungry Readings –
   Baker Books, North Dartmouth, MA
   Barnes and Noble Bookstores, North Dartmouth, MA

The Hallmark Nursing And Rehabilitation Center –
   New Bedford, MA

*In memory of Manuel E.
"Manny" Costa, Sr., social justice advocate,
criminal injustice fighter, historian, teacher,
athlete, coach, godfather and friend,
who in so many stand-up and giving ways
was the best of what is good about
this city.*

"Yo'!"

*And for Constance Mello
whose encouragement and support
led directly to the writing of
some of these poems.*

Contents

THIS CITY
  12 At The Hurricane Barrier
  13 This City: A Catalog
  16 On Johnny Cake Hill: A Sonic Vision
  18 Jamming
  19 At East/West Beaches
  20 Celebration

BLOOD'S RITE
  26 Blood's Rite

JUST WORDS
  34 Parting Ways:
  38 Paul Cuffee: Indian Blood
  43 Just Words: Frederick Douglass, 1838
  46 The Black Revisionist at the Blue Moon Café
  47 The Poet Laureate at the Bus Terminal
  48 Overheard in "New Beige":
  49 B. A. C. O. N. and Beans

STILL LIFE
  54 Still Life: An E 267 Exercise
  56 Many Thousand - Thousand Gone
  58 The "To Serve and Protect" Blues
  61 "But Then, Again,": The Reversal
  63 "Jerusalem! Jerusalem!!..."
  65 . . . Here . . .
  67 Herein

*I am a poor pilgrim of sorrow...
Sometimes I don't know where to roam...
...But I've heard of a city called Heaven
And I've started to make it my home.*
—from a Negro Spiritual

*This is the city and I am one of the citizens,
whatever interests the rest interests me...*
—Walt Whitman, Song of Myself

THIS CITY

At The Hurricane Barrier

Something there is that doesn't love a wall…
— Robert Frost, Mending Wall

Something in us all loves a wall, a fence,
partition, boundary, closed form, fixed space,
borders, territory. Something in each and all

of us gives a dam majesty, meaning, power.
Something within every western one likes to view
The Acushnet, Nile and unspent, dusky
Amazon pent-up and aching.

But something else in all of us wants it
breached, busted, broke. Something in us all
wants clothes off, rules and roles lifted, class down,

hookyed, races mixed, religion rent asunder
and loves an outlaw. Something in there
where its dark first feels better about it-

self when it sees others without, down and
dirty, and then ashamed of or for him or her,
itself and all of us. Something deep in

our keep knows why some caged things return free-
will to their opened cages — or never leave.
Something in us all fears a storm surge, loves

a wall and keeps it up and needs caging.
Other things inside us build battlements, erect
steep castles, locked temples, palatial places

to secure protection from the rhythm
of the river's rising
tides of change
without,
with-
in.

THIS CITY: A CATALOG

Cross-bloodied Native People
who named themselves
Massachusetts, became extinct.
Abolition's righteous Yankee
Quakers rose, addressed "The Light"
in subway tunnels'
blubber candles,
life-lit lanterns,
and smelled the sea in perfumes, sperm
whale blood, city coopers'
barrels of ambergris.
Negro Freedmen's gingerbread
latticed houses, glass works'
fires,
genteel plate cups, spindled women,
warehoused bosses,
cancer-causing dyeing vats,
Mill Street money,
banks and lawyers,
Wamsutta Club.
Earth-toned Crioulos,
earnest migrants,
Ernestina,
the tail end of whaling;
costly Coast Guard cutters chased rum runners
to The Smuggler's Den.

A hundred years of heavy fishing
—the Good Year's—
Belgium Congo forced labor camps,
rubber tires, tools and
golf balls… Factory owners migrate southward:
fishing flounders, high unemployment,
highs from tainted needles,
antique prison,
under aided A. I. D. S. programs,
sub-standard Red Cross colored cabs to nowhere;

the half-lit host of homeless sleep
in boarded storefronts, empty houses,
the too few full shelters;
addicted ancient adolescents are
cornered...
at Purchase and Hazard Streets,
near children's laughter
in pit bull playgrounds.
In kaleidoscopic stained glass pain,
needy parents kneel on
fine stitched prayer stools,
plead for gambling
and have casino dreams.
But the Kings of Keno
toast themselves by the hearth
in the gold domed State House
and coarsely chuckle at the despair,
down where our gritty city's people
are their funneled sand grains
in that Beacon Hilltop mansion's
marble mantel's hand blown hour
glass turned over and
over and over into perpetuity, until we are
turned...

Still, we in this working class city
with too little
work, smile and greet each other warmly
on the gull gray streets, sweep our outside
steps, stoops and porches, trim red wine vines
inside cyclone fencing, caringly
cultivate kale and kids, keeping them in,
sea wall them from the national storm surge
of remorseless militia, gang banging
and bad Bloods' sin.

Still, sun yellow dandelions
crack our old-time slate sidewalks,
upwardly seeking Their Source,
in this city of extraordinarily generous, super-
friendly, ordinary people who never let a neighbor
or stranger starve.

This city with a linguica-flavored lingua franca,
where a city hall, library, and church gave birth
to an art museum. This up-from-down
town of a city is itself a still life
museum of watercolored, olive oiled,
earth toned, one-pot boiled dinner
folk, feasting in mind and manner,
on faith, hope, charity, civility–old New
Bedford's best.

This richly storied, whale-taled, well oiled, shuttled,
tie-dyed city knitted between the clicking tips
of harpoons and today's tainted needles.
This city woven with the woof and warp
of threaded blood-ties and knotted genes,
this uniquely mixed-up Northeastern American city
asserts itself as a message to the world
in each of our many sunshine children's
raceless faces: Latino, Cape Verdean, Afro
American, Portuguese, dark white, light
black, colored???????? Who can tell? Today
this praying city where freedom-loving-
light-following Friends preyed upon whales,
where fishing flourished and fishing floundered;

this city of all humankind's faces shows
there is only one race:
The Human Race. A fact
more important than blood-inked scripture,
rusty harpoons, carved whale bones, cotton
looms, dry dye vats, tools, tires, fish count,
shell size, rope works or game balls.

Most magnificently of all, this all
too human city
manifests that worldly, cosmic fact.

ON JOHNNY CAKE HILL: A SONIC VISION

I leave the hollow rib cage
of the whale's skeleton
in the museum on Johnny Cake Hill.

My own echoing footsteps
break the silence throbbing on
my ear drums.

Outside in the foggy day
the doleful foghorn's pulsing
wails roll up from the waterfront,
regular as waves. There is a break-
down by the curb of the quaint re-cobbled
stoned street.

I assist a tourist, owner
of a fluke-tailed, white Cadillac
that is overheated, spouting steam,
parked on the other side

of the headlong road a whole nation's
taken to Profits Point. The owner
complains about his energy eating car
but brags,

"It's got a smooth transmission.
Listen to…"
the mechanical melody,
a whale's song modulated,
the desperate sonar of an endangered
species.

The unseen stream of sperm whale oil*
transmits a message. The whale's
sonic vision bounces off the soul's
ear. I hear blues; the desperate sonar

of an endangered species floats up
from the bandstands and jukeboxes
of waterfront cafes.

A palpable truth rises from these
sea-green blues like ambergris,
like Queequeg's coffin.
As we push the car to
the Whaling City Shell station,

the whole world is held fast
to my ear, like a sea shell,
in which I hear dying seas
and the extinction of singing things,
including us, in the cash register's

sounds, the mechanics of modulation.

*Note: Until relatively recently, some automatic transmission fluid contained oil derived from sperm whales.

JAMMING

It was that rainy summer night
when Bobby Greene was playing at The Pub.
He took out his horn
did his *thang*
and poured blue
milk into her ear.

She leaned near
and whispered to me.
It was the vaporous voice
of sax.

We picked up on the jam session
and danced home
to do it to death:

a duet to Life.

We sang all songs.
We danced all dances
until dawn came

up like song
on Sunday.

Dawn had a rainbow
wrapped around its waist,
and the pot
at the end of the rainbow
spilled over with

the alto rain of sax
and the baritone love-moan
of a saxophone:

At East/West Beaches

for Nia

The day night was born

we searched for rare,
old, sea-smoothed fragments of blue
and green bottles. Glass
made from sand made from stone
made from rock made
from cosmic dust.

We took off our shoes
and fringed the lips of under-
tow with footprints the waves
redeemed from the firm, wet
shore. We gathered and gave each other
milk white moonstones,
smooth surfaced obsidian,
pebbles translucent as sucked rock
candy and rolled up our jeans in the raw

salty mist. The sun sank into
a violet-lipped quahaug, and grit-edged night
opened like a mussel.
By black light we
crossed over a sandbar
into camp ground.

The night day was born
we turned around and found
no footprints.

CELEBRATION

I. Lest we forget

every Fourth of July
I want some country, some-
one to send a replica of one of all
those slave ships over the Middle
Passage to the tall ship parade—
to keep it honest, to make it real.

Remember them
moored at the waterfront steps
of Newport's fabled mansions?

...From under the rainbow, and through
our own Hurricane Barrier,
with storms in their wakes,
came the Portuguese *Sangue,* the Spanish, French, English,
Dutch and Yankee entries
and then slowly, slowly, slowly
came the *Lord Ligonier,* with a hold full
of Roots, after the *Esperanza* and *Jesus*
and with a cargo of allusive scrimshaw

on human bones...

A tide of blood recedes
exposing skeletons
and hand-carved bone crosses
pressed in the middle of Bibles
and history books.

II.

Scrimshaw. Beside me
bops Sister redbone love:

We embrace as history and future. We
walk along and up
but not away from the "Deep River"
our voices speak of.

She smiles all over
home where the blues are
somewhere between the greens
and the cornbread.

III. Communion...

Let us break bread together
on our knees, on our knees.
Let us break bread together
on our knees.

Love as bread
cast upon the waters...
Let us look away from obsidian mirrors,
and after you sang so loudly in church.
How you do the dough.
Juju and Jesus root
through your hands. Roots,
needing the kneading heart
beats from the lips;

sing the song sister!!

Blood's in this cornbread,
corn in the bread, Baby,
sun in the corn, and a
son of Africa in the cornucopia eyes
looking this way is how you
rite a bread
with dough so blushed with song
baked hot with mandated melanin
requisite to taste
this place's air.
There is a pestle and a gourd about
the act of kneading the tacky ova
of grain stained with sun.

Your cornbread.
The only blonde thing about you
gets down in the shiney baking pan
is a tambourine to glory
up into the oven as germ to womb...

Little bullied beans, blackeyed, punched out,
swell as syphons of the sauce

distilled from a swine whose funky soul
sacramentally
dances in the potted primal ooze and
around his own severed feet and side
steps as bacon drippin's in the chorus of
collards
on the amen corner of the stove
holy rollin'
'cause cookin' is a kind of dance done
with the hands and heart.

Your stone-ground stirrin' countershakes
it, makes it fecund and arousin';
it is hotly kissed by fire bakes it,
and we takes it.

Amen!

BLOOD'S RITE

Blood's Rite

for Kamal
(Based on a traditional African ritual)

CHARACTERS
A young (teenaged) black man
The young man's father
An old, grandfatherly Griot
Three young (teenaged) women dancers
Conga drummers and other drummers
The audience constitutes the village population

SETTING:
A manhood initiation ritual in the center of a traditional African village (a darkened platform, stage or floor). Everyone is wearing elegant traditional African attire for the high occasion. The young man is dressed in green; his father is dressed in blues; one young woman is dressed in red, another in black, another in green. The old man is dressed in gold.

Percussive instruments made of dried gourds containing seeds are given out to members of 'the village' along with other rhythm-keeping instruments.

There are three coconut palm trees, each with two coconuts, behind the platform.

GRIOT
(His voice from the darkness) The definition of what we are is that we are alive or that we have blood. A man will say that the fact that his sister has a monthly flow is a testament to Life that she is a bearer in the garden from which children come. So, traditionally a brother must show the union between him and his sister. When he reaches three weeks before his twelfth birthday he will cut his arm once for each sister that he has. So as the sister sheds blood on a monthly basis the brother cuts himself. The brother cuts himself on his arm to draw blood to show the bond between him and his sister. So God, to us, is The Life Stream or the continuation of the family, as such, the ancestors. A brother who fails to protect his sister will be put out of the house and the last name of his family is taken from him so that he has no contact or link with the ancestors.

(Drum music begins softly)

Three weeks before the twelfth birthday of the oldest brother the family will build a platform in the center of the village and all the people in that village will be assembled around that platform for his testimony.

(Lights up dimly on the Griot who is bathed in a purple spotlight)

GRIOT
I am the oldest man in the village, the one closest to our ancestors. This is a great day. For this is a day that is a day that has not been since Bundi passed this way. For this is the day on which a boy child will become a man child. Today is a day on which he will say a thing which we will hear. He will make known a deed that we shall obey. He will declare an act that we shall obey, for this is the day of the man child. Behold the boy child come. Make way for the boy child so that the man child might be heard.

(The people open a path and the boy and his father walk through to the Griot)

FATHER
(To the Griot and the village) I am here for this is the place where the people are. I am here because my ancestors are here. I am here because my son is here. I am here because this is the place where my man child must be. And so it is to this place that with my man child I have come. For this is the day of my man child and today I am.

SON
(To his father) Will today yield?

FATHER
Tomorrow must be heard so today will stand aside.
(Father exits into the darkness)

SON
(To the Griot) Will you yield that I might be heard?

GRIOT
(While circling the youth three times) There are three shadows in life. There is the shadow that is, the shadow that was, and the shadow that has yet to be. If the shadow that is has stood aside, then the shadow that was must, like life, fade away.
(Exits walking backwards into the darkness)

Son
(Faces the village) People of this village hear me
People of this village listen unto me
People of this village hear me
For I will say this thing one time
And yet I will say it the second time
On the day my sister marries
And the third time you will hear it
Will be on the day I will do this thing

Behold my sisters *(They are now in a gold spotlight)*
Behold my sisters but beware of my sisters

(Drum music becomes martial)

Beware of my sisters
For my sisters and I are one

(The sisters are dancing in a way that interprets the meaning of the son's lines)

Where my sisters walk—there I walk
Where my sisters stand—there I stand
Where my sisters sit—there is the place of my shadow
And where my sisters recline—there is the assurance of my honor

If it is in friendship that you have touched my sisters
then know that my friendship and honor are yours
But if it is in violence that you have touched my sisters
then be assured that in violence I will surely touch you
If you have put a mark on my sisters
I will put two for the one
If in violence you have spilled the blood of my sisters
If in violence you have caused the blood of my sisters to
fall to the earth
It matters not to me the reason or the cause my sisters may
have given you

(The drums are even more insistent at this point)

If in violence you have spilled their blood
whether it be from lip or nostril
You have in violence brought down my sister's blood
to the earth
I will demand your life for my sister's blood
Or *(Points East into the darkness)* I will answer

To my ancestors in The World Beyond The Mist
For the cause of my failure

(Drum rhythms become appropriate for a procession)

And if I fail this oath is binding upon my brothers
For the men of this house are one

(Two brothers from the audience, dressed in African garments, walk with spears to where the sisters are dancing, and then the brothers stand in honor guard fashion)

And if my brothers fail
Then my cousins will come

(Cousins, two of them, do same as the brothers)

For the men in this house are one
And if my cousins fail
My father will come

(Father does same as cousins)

For the men in this house are one
And if my father fails
Then my uncles will come

*(Two more men come over to the sisters
The men all carry spears
They line up in twos)*

For the men in this house are one
And if my uncles fail
Then my grandfather, bowed by his age and the grey hairs of his beard
yet the old man will come

(Griot does the same as the men before him)

For the men in this house are one

And if my grandfather fails
Then will the spirit of the ancestors smile upon the women

(The sisters take spears from three of the above male and then dance militaristically)

That the women may be mightier than the men
And on that day the women will come

(All of the people in the action shout as a chorus:)

FOR ALL IN THIS HOUSE ARE ONE!!!

Hear me then and hear me well
Beware of my sisters
Beware of my sisters for my sisters are a gift
To me from my ancestors
They are the assurance from yesterday to today
That there will be a tomorrow
For how shall a people be
But a brother shall have a sister
Who he lends to a strange family
So that she brings forth fruit to that family tree
From out of the sister must come all generations to be

Behold mine
Behold mine that you may know her
And know her that you may beware of her
Beware lest you touch her
For none shall touch my sister
Save he I choose he who pleases me
And it pleases me that, in violence, no one
Not even the hand of my father shall descend upon my sisters

(Spotlight on Father who nods 'yes')

Behold my sisters
Behold my sisters for my sisters and I are one
Beware of my sisters lest you touch them
For it will be the touch that will kill you

GRIOT
(Walks back to the young man, looks at him, and walks around him three times and says as he does so:)
Once for yesterday, once for today, and once for tomorrow — for all things are in cycles of three. *(He regards the young man with mock disdain)* Such words from a little one! How do we know you are a man child? How do we know that this is not a boy who speaks such things before men? How know we that you are a manchild? Prove that you are a manchild!

SON
(Assertively) By Bundi you shall know it is true.

GRIOT
Eh! So you know of Bundi, do you? Then tell us of Bundi so that we will know your words are true

SON
(There is a kaleidoscopic swirl of lights)
In the time when time was not
By the place where place was not
From out of the river where the river was not
From out of the water where water was not known
From out of the mud where mud was not
Came forth life
And Life was Bundi
And Bundi was Blood
And Blood was life

And so as it was the blood of my father
So it was the Blood of his father
And his father's father
And as my sister sheds by month the blood
That is Life
It is the bond that is Bundi

Behold the blood bond *(He 'cuts' his arm once for each of the three sisters and the whole stage is bathed in red light)*

GRIOT
(To the village) We have heard and having heard we have seen. For blood is Life and we have seen the blood, and, so, it is Bundi, and we know that Bundi passed this was. (In forbidding tones) Therefore, you will obey. For if you fail, your family will not stand with you after you have touched his sister, and your family will not remember you when he comes, for this is the way of a manchild.

SON
(Surrounds himself with his sisters; the sisters form a triangle)
Where is the shield of my sisters?!

(All the male characters invoked in his speech form, by twos, a human spear. The sisters and the son constitute the pointed head of it. They walk away toward and through the audience, up the center aisle and out of sight.)

THE END

© copyright 1970,1976,1997

JUST WORDS

PARTING WAYS:

Notes and thoughts at Parting Ways Cemetery

The sign reads:

> *Parting Ways Cemetery*
>
> *Here Lie The Graves Of Four Negro Slaves -*
> *Quamany - Prince - Plato - Cato -*
> *These men fought in The Revolutionary War*
> *and were freed at its close.*
> *The cemetery is located in the original 94 acre lot*
> *deeded to them by the government*
> *when they were given their freedom.*

Manumission: Death, the Great Emancipator.

The wind and rain are part of a wreath
of wildflowers and weeds and blackberry
vines. Remnants of an ancient dwelling's
foundation, half a field away,
an archeological dig—strings, stakes—excavates
the old Colony of New Guinea.

They are always trying to dig us,
always trying to dig either our essence
or our grave.

Black-Eyed Susan holding Queen Anne's Lace
mauve blossoms I do not know
blood and blues make purple.

Weathered, grey granite. Five grassless graves.
Blight, rust, bracket fungi on
hickory, oak, maple, sycamore,
conifers, sumacs, poison ivy
and many, many vines.

A twin trunked oak sucks
seeks downward.
Roots. The vines are potted in
five skulls think
blackberries. To eat one is to

chew on a dream, to swallow
the sweet thought of hope. The berries

are succulent ball shot,
pigmented hopes, tears
from underground, ball bearings
from a subway train:

Quamany, Prince Goodwin, Plato Turner, Cato Howe.
Jefferson, Washington, Franklin:
the premiere founding fathers in
The American Pantheon —
two slave holders and an inventive lecher,
from places named after
virginity and brotherly love.

They tell us: *Do not as I do;*

do as I say do.
Franklin belly-flopped his way through France
after the womb-shaped
Sound of Philadelphia
was cracked by hypocrisy:
the tolled alloy of our mettle.

II.
Quamany, Prince, Plato, Cato.

So you fought. We be
fighters.

Did you ever see Plymouth rock?
It boogys now, from the beat
of a death rattle -
"I tremble... when I remember God..."

Plymouth Rock, America's
specious touchstone.

The footsteps turned to gold
"...follow the yellow brick road"

The yellow brick Catholic
school, down the road, and around the corner,
was also founded on rock-
hard Peter

met Pocahontas, Malintzin, Maimiti
and the girls of Guinea—
our mothers, sisters, wives
or daughters.
*Yankee Doodle went to town, riding
on a pony...*

Washington's monument is not monolithic,
is really a corkscrew,
the sheepherders spirocyte,

Franklin's diplomacy.

Spirals. The vine winds
down day dreams,
rain drops
filter through
summer leaves bathe the berries.
Fall. Will come
with trees of fire.
America will flame with Fall.
Fire — the alchemist's purifier.

The Melting Pot is pestle and mortar.

That is why Yankee Doodle tries
to yodel the blues -

*"Oh say can you see
by the dawn's early light..."*

Jefferson's jitters, a death rattle:
*"...all men are created equal...
Oh Sally, hold me! ...I tremble
for my country when I remember
God is just."*

III.
Quamany, Prince, Plato, Cato,

Soldiers of Fortune. Freedom, the inalienable right, was
fought for.
We be fighters.

So you fought. For what?
To help make independent

a system set to enslave your
sons and their sisters for another century.

You meant well. Were trying to survive.
Believed in, hoped for the self-evident promise.
Had good intentions
line the yellow brick road.

You could not vote but
you fought. We be fighters.

Two hundred years.
Today Black people are picking berries
for big business, in a bog,
not far from here.
Bushels of Blackness.
Quarts of tears.

Massachusetts did not even
want to give you this
sign, this cemetery, had to be fought for,
beside a road
that is now backed up with brick-
yellow school buses.
We be fighters.

IV.
The wind weaves a wreath
of weeds, wildflowers
and blackberry ballshot.

The wind weaves my
cigarette smoke, a ghost
vine.
The wind is a wreath of words:
"...all men are created equal..."

The wind... four rusty muskets.

V.
This visit was only as long
as two cigarettes.
Both snuffed butts
stained with dream

is scrimshaw on your bones

PAUL CUFFEE: INDIAN BLOOD

I. POOCUTOHHUNKUNOOK:

Coffee black Akan. Wampanoag woman.
Grey wind,
gulls.
Grey rock,
grey sea. Scuds.
Poocutohhunkunook

Cuffee Slocum, Ruth Moses. Spume and
the slate grey sea births
Paul, John, Freelove, seven more.
Black and red on grey.

Grave. *Death is manumission.*
Father dead, farm dead
Fish don't fertilize rock, Jesus'
good seed will make
a fisherman out of me.

John Cuffe: "Farm the sea?"

Brother, farm the shark grey sea.

Sixteen. Common seaman spermwhaling.
Gulf of Mexico. West Indies.
Reads, writes first
words
are quilled scrimshaw on white skull bones.

White war. Blacks serve.
Five-thousand gone. War is
Manumission.

Cuffee pays dues but not taxes.
Massachusetts Constitution 1778:
"males... excepting Negroes, Indians
and Mulattoes, shall be entitled to vote."
Paul petitions and petitions
and petitions
and teaches

a life rite called
The Yankee.
Civil disobedience in Westport way before Walden.
Jail.

Ties up in a red Wampanoag
harbor.
Alice Pequit. His mother's mirror.

Twenty-five. Master of a *small covered vessel*
of twelve tons.
Home is west shore of East River,
Below Hix's Bridge, Westport.
Good wharf, good woods.
Sure shipbuilding. Vessels.

1787. *Three-fifths of a man?*
Seaman, sperm-whaling
master of a small covered vessel
of two sons.

1791. Santo Domingo. Industrial Revolution.
Northern negroes hassled.
Free negroes in New York left homeless.

John Cuffee Writes sister Freelove:
"Why do the colored run after the whites
and join their churches?
It helps to keep negroes in slavery."

In the City of
Friends Absalom Jones and Richard Allen say,
Amen.

Friend Paul Cuffe
sees the light at Acoaxet, 1808
No nigger pew for me.
No nigger pew for me.
The Quaker grey sea.

With Friends help
business booms. Many vessels
from Boston to Savannah.

Grey sea leads to gold coast.

II. SERR LYOA:

Land of Africans, free blacks from Nova Scotia
and many, many emigrated Jamaican Maroons—
Fierce Bloods.

Cuffe solicits Philadelphia Friends.
Funds for "enlightenment process" in Africa.
He plots to bring freed Bloods back
to homeland over century before Garvey.
Abolitionists go for it.
Manumission from guilt.

1811. Favorite ship, *Travellor,*
carries Cuffee from cold
grey to molten golden light, Africa,
28th February.
Harbor: Freetown, Governor: Columbine.

African seed did well in the kernel of
an *Indian*
corn grows well in Serr Lyoa.

Met the Bullone. The Mandingo are Muslims,
educated in arabic… no rum praise God!

Some London backers want liquor imported.
Cuffee: *No!*

Paul petitions and petitions
and petitions.
Teaches a long, long
dance with the dollar.
Dance called the Yankee.

Takes on four African navigation apprentices.
Teaches them to Yankee.
Sails for Liverpool.

1811. *Edinburgh Review:*
"Ship with black owner, master, mate, and crew
lands in a port, lately, the nimbus of the slave trade."

April, 1812. Home. White waμμr. Travellor seized
because barrel of French brandy aboard.
Madison releases ship after meeting with Cuffee.

No nigger pew for me.

Dolly Madison helps equip ship for next trip East.
Ice cream and Christ for the Africans.

December, 1815. *Travellor* sails, pointed dead
at the dawn.
Tobacco, soap, candles, naval stores, thirty-eight
(mainly Boston)
black artisans and laborers, flour, iron, a wagon
and a plow.

Travellor sails on a sea of blood.
More than two-hundred ships go to Africa
this year for slaves.

White southerners fear insurrections
a decade and a half since Gabriel had done the do.

The whites create their own instruments of execution
is manumission.

February, 1816. *Leonine mountains.* New governor,
MacCarthy, admired Jefferson's dusky Sally,
and has mulatto mistress, Hannah Hayes.
Ashanti will do the do on him in 1824.

Blacks are back where they want to be.
Manumission.

Cuffee plans short stay:
I must leave you in HIS hands… Farewell.

April, 1816. Grey hair under the wig. Sails home.
Camwood and squills.
Poor sales.
Trip shortens Cuffee's Yankee
dance with the dollar.

Americans plan for a "mercantile Line"
of business, for the *Travellor,*
on their silver dollar sea
from New England to Africa. *In the fawl.*
Paul Cuffee's emigration concept
cause celebre.
Samuel J. Mills, American Colonization Society:

"We must save the Negroes for the Negroes will ruin us."

III. MANUMISSION

September 7th, 1817. Captain Cuffee deathly ill.
Doctor bill $33.98 (paid)
Petitions PHYSICIAN for another day.

September 8th he is fifty-eight;
a black gull breaks free of his rib cage,

going to a world of joy, A Shining World!
Poocutohhunkunook. Through God's sea grey eye,
the sky,
manumission.

JUST WORDS:
FREDERICK DOUGLASS, 1838

I am a poor pilgrim of sorrow…
Sometimes I don't know where to roam…
…But I've heard of a city called Heaven
And I've started to make it my home.

Dead Fred Douglass alive
in the after-life of The Word:

…no more
driver's lash for me, no more,
no more…
The gospel train's a-comin'.
I hear it rumblin' through the land.
The poorest of poor can go,
with their fare in hand;
the fare is faith and struggle.
So what we waitin' for? Get on board,
Children, there's room for many a-more.

"If there is no struggle, there is no progress…"

Just words in hand, on borrowed free
merchant seaman's papers loaned
by brother Freeblood. Given
meager money and abundant love,
in Baltimore your freedom financed by fiancée,
free born Anna Murray, who
risking all, would marry you
on a side-track at a way station.

And, so, wearing her heart's handiwork,
disguised as a sailor in a blood red shirt,
tarp hat, black cravat, you boarded the train
in Maryland at Mercy Station, north-
bound to Jubilee Terminal,
where you would be

free.

*Board! Children get on Board!! There's room
for many a-more!* On the overground
railroad by train- by ferry (and very nearly
betrayed by Tomming)- but, back aboard
by train- by steamboat- by train to New York City,
up from down
South, our Old Country.

Brother Fugitive, his job search white wash
brush in hand, helped you, hipped you
to dangers afoot from bounty
hunters. Alone you sought the familiar
waterfront.

Free,

but homeless and hungry, you slept amid
the boxed Brown's, coopers' copper and molasses barrels
on a wharf. You dreamt of caulking
Liberty's cracked bell.

Later, hidden and housed by yet another
sympathetic sailor, unlike

"…those who want the ocean without the roar
of it's many waters…,"

you were conducted to underground station
master, Ruggles, in whose home you were joyfully
joined at heart to Anna by The Right Reverend Runaway,
by
just

words, providentially guided to Newport,
on a cold, open steamship deck wedding
night, with a gold ring around the harvest moon.
Once there, where without
New Bedford stagecoach fare, you fared well,
with city's Friends Taber and Ricketson:

Get Thee in and fare Thee well!!

Horse drawn to the end
of your new beginning of what will
be your life-long end.

...FREE, at last...

in standup Brother Nathan Johnson's house,
Old First Friend's Meeting, at Mercy's
Well Spring and Seventh Heaven Streets
in old New Bedford Village.
On that Great Gettin' Up Mornin', where
barely there you are
re-renamed. You'd been
bound as Bailey, journeyed as Johnson,
and by Nathan's reading of a poem —

just words, at your overground under-
ground train trip's last stop, steeped
in words, baptized in purpose you came
roaring out of Nathan Johnson's door,
reborn lean and leonine Frederick Douglass
of the life-long, reasoned, rhetorical roar:

"Power concedes nothing without a demand;
it never did and it never will."

The still reverberating roar
tells those content to quietly wait
for justice,
Don't leave life to chance or fate!

"Agitate! Agitate!! Agitate!!!"

Your roar reminds us
who we have been and should be:
Fred Douglass
in the afterlife of his words:

...I've heard of a city called Heaven
And I've started to make it my home.

The Black Revisionist at the Blue Moon Café

...Oh, yeah? Listen, Brother:
Man, what was Crispus Attucks thinking, with
his little huckle-buckle shoe,
knee-stocking and knee breech wearing-
self,
outside a tavern, unarmed and half-
drunk, in the middle of a mob
of wine-faced, ale-assed, Colonial
Bostonians, their spilling tankards in hand,
selling wolf tickets to a rank
of Red Coats with bayonetted muskets
aimed dead at his heart?

Man what was Crispus Attucks thinking?
With his little huckle-buckle shoe,
holey knee-stocking, knickerbocker, and
torn shirt wearing, knapsack-toting, runagate,
just-found-freedom self?!

And that postage stamp
tribute to Buffalo Soldiers.
Bloods paid to capture San Juan Hill
or to kill, guard or hassle Indians.
Man, many "red skins" had taken us in,
gave sanctuary from the ruthless, common foe.
Back then many a Black man's friend, grandma,
mama or wife was Indian.

You got to wonder about colored folk
who get the oke-doke, get commemorated,
feel honored, for killing one another.

Only telling you what God loves, Brother:
the truth. Yo! Don't Go, Bro'!!

The Poet Laureate at the Bus Terminal

Yo' ! Pro' !! It's your boy,
LeRoy.

Hey, Bro'. You know,
the newspaper, other day,
say you being honored.

But Pro' ! ! How's it show?
Now, I know you been po'.

But, yo', wha's up with the city
callin' you a po' it
and low-rate, too? You know?
How's the honor show?

He leaned into that "Yo'
lend-a-me-a-dollar" look.

Do you get any dough?

I said, No.
He said,

Oh.
So, that's being po'
it, low-rate.
O.K., man. Now I understand.

Overheard in "New Beige":

God made the black man
and the white man; Portugal
made the mulatto.

B. A. C. O. N. AND BEANS

for the Frederick Douglass Unity House at UMass Dartmouth

Black,
Afro American,
Colored, Creole, Caribbean,
Or,
Negro,
"We are therefore I am;
I am because we are"*
a new people on the world:

indio, mestizo, negro, mulatto, quad-
roon, negrindian,
a variegated, earth-toned music-
al people. In all the Americas,
the Antilles and old Cabo Verde.

In Africa, we were
self-named with our own tongues: The People,
The People Who…, The People From…,
The People By…

…By the by, the wakes
of the slave schooners split our tongues,
in the hold belly-to-back-to-belly,
stowed like galley spoons, we were forked
into new folk, a creolized continuum.

Called out of our names by our captors:
Prete, Swartz, Noir, nigger, made
by inhumanity, we are
a new five-hundred year old people
in the world.
By barque and barracoon,
octoroon,
Borinquen, Kriolu, Latino,
ununited and tribal
to a fault, in the name of diversity.

Ancestral spirits say,
"Sticks in a bundle are unbreakable"**
Not one of us is truly free
unless all of us are truly free, together.

Free to tell
each other
what we call ourselves, free

to talk shit and eat Brie
at ever so correct collegiate affairs,
where we put on airs. Or free to mend,
to choose our own coalition friends,
our own politics and poetics, free
to realize the necessary unity. Can't you see
Kinte cloth is woven with the warp and woof
of many colors. All that is

different are the cultures, the words
of our conquerors and colonizers. We all
make rice and beans by similar means
but with different spices.

**from Dr. John Mbiti's* African Religions and Philosophy
***an African proverb*

STILL LIFE

Still Life: An E 267 Exercise

Note — Those of us in my Introduction To Poetry Writing
  Workshop walked the inner sidewalk circle of the UMass
  Dartmouth campus, and each of us "sketched" something
  from the shared experience to craft toward poetry.

We walk the cement inner circle
sidewalk, predefined, rigid
as a verse form, in view of privilege,

a brief schooled excursion to cite
exhibitions of class, to sight Blake's
angel's pained face pressed against a science
building's picture window. The motion of poetry

proceeds on the padded paws of night-time's
tyger, the cave bear of primal fear,
the heightened heartbeat, high pressured im-
pulse of Poetry stalks and preys upon us. Use
Caution: pedestrian poetry ahead. We

break to smoke or talk or write
but not for the ritual gift
of mined salt, not for the grain flour
formula, not for bread broken like marriage
vows and treaties. We come back, over

and over, again, to wars and weddings,
full circle to their ceremonial solemnity,
their joys, bells and jail bars. The cyclical
milling motion of history. The migrations
of our ever-less-kind kind's on-going
exodus out of The Edenic Rift
Valley toward "owning" Ever-Ever Land
are circular. All our auras, halos, cast gold promise
rings, like retold tales weighed down by round
campfire stones, are meant to secure, protect

us from the cyclical darknesses:
loneliness, war, death, broken circles.

And, so, we walk the "universal",
university path back over the state of things, over
and over again, with monotonous metonymy.
Our feet keep the lyric
beat of a round,
the concrete prosody of politics, as iambs in
the empirical poetry of empire.

MANY THOUSAND - THOUSAND GONE

for Reza

(Re: The 1980's Atlanta child murders)

Nathanial, Latonya, Christopher... They are not just figures,
not just numbers; they are our heartbeats. Let us say their names:

Edward, Alfred, Milton, Yusef, Angel, Eric, Tony,
Earl Lee, Clifford, Charlie, Aaron, Terry, Patrick, Jeffrey,
Curtis, Timmy, Eddie, Larry
Joseph, Michael, Jimmy, William, Darron...

Twenty-seven, twenty-eight?
Though one would have been
too many, how many children
cried and died on the trek in chains?
How many soon died of diet or shock
in the barracoons, like Gorée? How many
(stowed like stacked spoons, with no breathing
room, clutched in the *suffocating* hold
of the slave ship *Grim Reaper*) died
back there on Middle Passage?

How many with their last moans
"flew" home to Africa during the first soul-chilling snow
after auction block? How many
galloped away in the night
on a pale, red-speckled horse
called consumption? How many
tiny bundled ones *froze* or *burned* up
with fever in their parents' arms
on the Underground Railroad?

How many were forcibly *drowned*
in Charleston Harbor or Cape Fear River?
It kills and kills; how many
Emmett Tills have we had?
How many would-have-beens
have been *prevented from being*
because of involuntary sterilizations?

If it was or is just one child,
one would be too many.

So, who do you think it is?
Say, who could be this way?
Who is killing all these kids?

Who? Black or white, male or female.
the kid-killers are the ugly id
of America. It profited from its holdings
in slave ships. It got rich
off the quarters behind Mt. Vernon
and Monticello and from ghettos.
It waxed strong and fat
on cotton fields and blues.

WE HOLD THESE TRUTHS
TO BE SELF-EVIDENT:
Middle Passage, auction block,
black codes, Jim Crow, lynch law,
burning crosses, Sunday school
bombings, benign neglect, Medgar Evers,
Lester Lima, Martin Luther King.

What more is there to say
or ask or pray? Who
are the accomplices, accessories?
Those among us unwilling to change
a warping, stunting, killing system
that causes or profits from crack babies,
no needle exchange,
A. I. D. S.,
ghettoes, Middle Passage and the second Post-
Reconstruction.
But we go on treating symptoms instead of causes;
we go on killing all children
with pollution, deforestation,
the A. B. C's of PCB's
How many black children have been
killed? Though one was (and is)
too many–many, many

MILLIONS!!!

Millions marked by dozens,
millions by the score.
God! How many more…?

The "To Serve and Protect" Blues

Have you seen the obscene
photos of inhumanity?
He was killed. Just
died, they say
expertly,
of an overdose! Just

as he died over
and over, down
in the stinking, choking hold
of the slave ship *Gracia de Dios*... Just
as he died
a million X's
over the diaspora
choking on strange, blue fruit
from The Human Family Tree.

His own folk testify with *mornas*
over the sea-green-blues
of our history.

One way or another,
arrested,
he died in a jail cell
in a tradition, a custom:
protective custody.
At first he was
unwilling
then he wasn't

able to throw down,
throw up the evidence
of the swallowed crime.

The old, old ritual: whipping Boy.
Beaten
over and over
again
with snarls, sneers, jeers.

His still color
photo, bloody,
flattened face the face
of Emmett Till beneath
the still water.
The face of Rodney King
"Kong" still in the eyes
of the perpetrators.

Brother, one way or another
Morris Pina's telling Rorschach bruises
his misshapened head, body
bag
are
emblematic of the old cult's
id.
They give the lie to those
who
fairly say he died justly.

No. He was not
an Innocent. Neither was
he proven guilty. One way
or another
there is no life

sentence; there is no death
sentence in this state
of Massassippi
for the wrong-
ful death of a "…black
son-of-a-bitch!" Or Beantown's
old, sick, retired reverend, who
was scared to death in his living room
in a wrongful drug raid.

Over and over
again, the fears of Post-Reconstruction,
The Depression and Eisenhower years.
The temper, the tone,
the times bear it out, bare
the old ritual standard:

BLACK MAN IN CUSTODY DEAD

of an Overdose of Service and Protection.

Mark Furman's in his heaven.
Not just
in service blues.
Not just in Idaho. No.
He's camouflaged in local faces.

All's right with the good
Ol' U. S. of

eh?

"But Then, Again,": The Reversal

(For Matthew Eappen and all the unremembered, nameless, faceless children who have been battered or molested or murdered before, during and since the recent "Au Pair" cause celebre and whose abuse or deaths didn't get live coverage.)

Man, this "H" bus is crowded today. Say,
what's the news 'bout that nanny?
Man, if she'd a been a mammy
she'd a got the double-whammy.

Let me see that *Tribune*.
Man, I didn't think the judge would
come back so soon!
I wonder

if even
in Faire Olde New England
if fair
au pair Louise Woodward
would a been set free
if the dead child victim
had been blonde,
"All-American,"
 Little Miss-Directed,
Junior Barbie, Jeanne Benet Ramsey???

I don't know
but I don't think so.
But then, again, if
ya got it like that,
even if
convicted of manslaughter
of someone's baby daughter,
ya can get over, get off
with less time in The Joint
than our 19 year old kids get
for a joyride in somebody's Ford.

What's my "point?"

Point is she didn't get out just
behind 'reasonable doubt.'
It's also behind the old "Jail Bars
Blues." What did Lady Day
say? "Them that's got shall get."
Dig. If ya don't get ya people to unite
and throw down big time,
ya might as well be
guilty of the crime.

If ya don't get live
international t.v. here poured into

mom-and-pop Pub Culture pints of nut
brown beer
with thick, white, foaming heads,
ya may just get life! Or, death!!

If ya don't get world attention
to get the judge (a vase of baby's breath
and off-season English roses for the bench's side
bar)
to countermand the peerless jury
of the realm; if ya don't get

a satellite dish full of long bread
ya dead.
If ya don't get part of The Dream Team,
ya don't get O.J. "justice."
In the end
ya get The American Nightmare.

Get it? Ask Mumia!
This is my stop, man.
Good talkin' with ya.
I'll see ya. Oh, ya know
what's really lame?
We remember the nanny, but,

yo', what's the baby's name?

---

* *The Philadelphia Tribune* is an African American newspaper.

"Jerusalem!, Jerusalem!! ...

Hosanna in The Highest..." Hell
fire smoke soot
covered bodies
lay on the ground their
panic splashed water
melons' juices smashed brain matter
multitudes trampled blood-slicked news
paper shredded money green rinds
torn awnings foot mashed fishes
sandal prints on pieces broken hand
made love's unleavened loaves

Salaam scraps scraped
Shalom vestments dangle
downed telephone lines
tattered cloth star
crossed patterns
hang from the dripping
tip of the gold scimitar
shaped moon seeds limbs
bits of heavenly bodies
adorn The Day Star
over the wholly taken Holy Land

Nothing changes but the money

The Sacred City's many
honeyed words for locust
plagued underripe peace
fruit stalls turned
over
ripped wrapping paper
as in The Crusades
all wars are fought
over
real estate
in the worldly market place

The Ark of The Covenant's lease
is rent
in configurations of:
the crescent's arc
the star's triangles
the cross's planes

Pax again and again man
-made self-
willed amends with

Amen

. . . Here . . .

*(In memory of my great-grandmother,
Martha Prattis Nichols Brown,
who lived to be 111 years old)*

for Ayan

She rose from the rocker, unfolded
The Afro American article*,
pointed it out:

Lord!
This world's a mess! Folks fighting to be
called "Most Oppressed":

black folk, women folk, old folk.
Who's most oppressed? Me I guess.
Got it all, being
as I'm old, black woman.
But, so what? Whining never
got even a kid more than candy or
a pat on the head, nor a yard dog
a kick or a bone.

Struggle and strife are the facts of life.
Your hard working Grandpa's dead, but
you are the afterlife of his labor.
Our work has been our worship.

So, take our tattered, threadbare, patchwork
hope and work with it. Yes, kneel to God,
but stand up to people who fight your right
to the life God give you.

Some say 'home is where the heart is.'
That's true if heart is courage, strength and faith.
'Cause, in this life, home is wherever
your struggle is. And, son, the work's undone.

We just cleared the ground, plowed and planted;
the weeding, watering,
watching, waiting, the long work
is up to you. We ain't no ways through.

So, yes, keep the faith, but
keep the farm, too. Hold on
to home ground, and learn that living
should be learning, too. Remember
what Fred Douglass read and wrote for you,
and Robeson, your Malcolm X and Dr. King.

The main thing written clear
right 'mongst these headlines here:
the whole world's your home, hear? Here ...

*The name of a national African American newspaper

Herein

for Mayor Rosemary S. Tierney

*On the occasion of the
Sesquicentennial Time Capsule Interment Ceremony,
October 3, 1997*

As nearby trees flame with Fall,

here in the clear, sharp, high-pitched light
blues of earth-toned, harvest time's apple
crisp air, ...*We The People*... of New Bedford,
with reaper blade, rocker runner smiles
on New Moon Faces,

with faith in the fact of Spring,
in a black loam and pumpkin orange rite,
Yankee as yearly almanac
and ripe fruited apple trees,
we, that orchard's amber suede, bruised,
windfall, wine sap

apples, plant this hopeful seed
documenting our dusty days'
doings and deeds, commending it to you who
open it hereafter, and to That/Who beyond
our ken or keep, keeps all time unclocked
and rocks our cradled galaxy

asleep. With faith in the fact of Spring
we toast you in your mulled cider!
And celebrate you yearly in a rose
flurry of falling City Hall Japanese cherry

tree blossom petals.